Copyright © 2026 Kelly Reddin
Illustrations copyright © 2026 Kelly Reddin
All Rights Reserved

This is a work of fiction. Names, places, characters and incidents are either the product of the author's imagination or are used fictitiously, and any resemblance to any actual persons, living or dead, businesses, organizations, events or locales is entirely coincidental.

No part of this book may be reproduced or transmitted in any form or by any means, electronic or mechanical, including photocopying, recording, or by any information storage and retrieval system, without permission in writing from the author.

Library of Congress Control Number: 2025924157

Publishing Coordinator – Clarissa Willis
Book Design – Sharon Kizziah-Holmes

SOLANDER
— PRESS —

Springdale, Arkansas

Paperback ISBN: 978-1-966675-65-5
Hardback ISBN: 978-1-966675-64-8
eBook ISBN: 978-1-966675-66-2

I LOVE MY UNCLE

A Celebration of Uncles

I LOVE MY UNCLE
A Celebration of Uncles

written by
Kelly Reddin

illustrated by
Sommer J. Buyante

I love my Uncle. He had a cool car when he was in college. He would pick me up on weekends, and we would drive with the top down. We went on hikes, and he talked to me about growing up. Sometimes he brought his girlfriend with him. He showed me how to open doors and let her go first.

Once, the three of us drove bumper cars. We crashed, we banged, we got stuck. We laughed so hard our stomachs hurt. I love my uncle.

I love my Tio. He taught me to swim and to kayak. When I was little, he took me to a pool.

When I was older, we went kayaking on a river. He taught me to be safe on the water. We always wear lifejackets. We have so much fun getting wet going through rapids. Now we go kayaking every summer. I love my Tio.

I love my Anakala. He is a great surfer, and he taught me to surf and waterboard. He helps me check the forecast and read wave charts.

He picks me up after work, and we head straight to the beach. We surf for a couple of hours almost every day. We often see dolphins when we are surfing. Sunset on the water is awesome. I love my Anakala.

I love my Uncle. He gave me a tennis racket for my tenth birthday. We started just hitting the ball back and forth. Soon, we could play a real game. My serve was bad at first. With practice and a few tips, I got much better.

My Uncle comes to my high school tennis matches. He is my biggest fan. I love my uncle.

I love my Unk. He loves video games, and so do I. Mom makes fun of us sometimes, but she loves seeing her brother and me together.

Unk likes to play games where his character jumps, runs, spins, and grabs. Sometimes he shows me special codes. Sometimes I show him a special move. We play together and we play against each other. We talk about lots of stuff while we play. I love my Unk.

I love my Shushu. He trains dogs. I work with him on weekends at his dog academy. I help him set up the course and make sure we have plenty of water in the bowls.

I am learning how to train dogs so they can help people. He shows me how patience and perseverance help in all aspects of life. Someday, some of the dogs I help train will be service dogs. I am so proud of my Shushu, and I love him so much.

I love my Zio. We had a party for my eighth birthday at the bowling alley. They put bumpers on the sides so my ball would stay in the lane. When my Zio bowled, the bumpers weren't there. He threw so many strikes.

We had so much fun that we kept bowling every month. He helps me be a good winner and a good loser. Sometimes he takes me to leagues with him. My dad likes it when Zio and I spend time together. Dad and I love my Zio.

I love my Wujek. He is kind of quiet, but he really listens to me. I like to talk to him about good things and things that bother me. He gives me good advice. We cook special Polish dishes together. We talk, taste, and laugh.

My parents join us when the food is ready. My Wujek makes me feel so special. I love my Wujek.

I love my Uncle. He and I go deer hunting together. At first, I just watched. I had to be quiet and still. That was hard. Now I can use a bow, and we both can hunt.

We built a deer stand and use it when we go out. Sometimes we don't see even one deer. But when we do, we usually get at least one. We work together to field-dress the deer. The venison always tastes good. I love my Uncle.

I love my Uncle. He is a writer. He tells me lots of stories and reads many books to me.

He wrote several short stories for me and let me draw the pictures. He and I are making a book that contains the stories. My Uncle encourages me to write, so I try. He helps me make the stories better. He reads my stories and uses different voices for each character. He makes me laugh. I love my Uncle.

I love my Oji. He and I are learning to play golf. We started by playing miniature golf. We had so much fun. He bought two putters. Then, we went to the practice green. Next, he bought an iron and a wood. We went to the driving range, and each of us hit a bucket of balls. Most of the drives were ground balls. Oji called them "worm killers."

Eventually, we learned how to hit the ball high so it would go far. He found some golf clubs at a garage sale. Now we play on the golf course. We help each other find balls we hit in the rough. We laugh, talk, and have a soda at the end. I love my Oji.

I love my Uncle. He plays cornhole with me. He is really good. I am getting better. My Uncle can do anything.

He plays basketball with me. He makes a lot of baskets. He uses a wheelchair, but is a better player than many people who can jump and run. He teaches me that you can do anything if you practice and never give up. I love my Uncle.

I love my Uncle. He and I like to ride horses. We ride into the forest and through fields. My uncle tells me about the trees, the animals, and how to take care of the land.

He shows me how to brush and comb the horses. We work together and talk about what I might want to do when I am an adult. I love my Uncle.

Many people are lucky enough to have an uncle. An uncle creates memories through activities or just being together. An uncle's love is inside each one of their nephews and nieces. They are thankful for uncles who love them.

Do you have a special name for your uncle? What do you and your uncle do together? What special memories have you made with him?

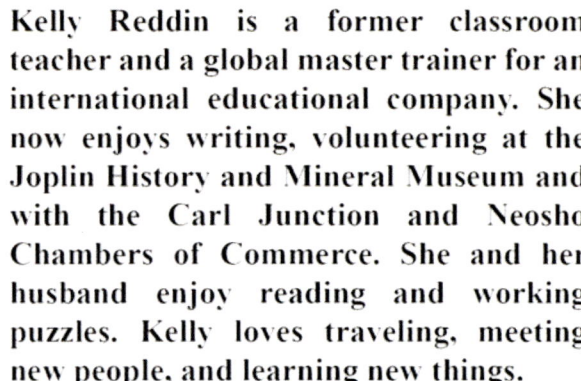

Kelly Reddin is a former classroom teacher and a global master trainer for an international educational company. She now enjoys writing, volunteering at the Joplin History and Mineral Museum and with the Carl Junction and Neosho Chambers of Commerce. She and her husband enjoy reading and working puzzles. Kelly loves traveling, meeting new people, and learning new things.

Be sure to join Kelly's mailing list to get updates on new publications and events.

Sommer J. Buyante was born and raised where the sea meets the sky in Palawan, Philippines. At 26, she has found her calling in the world of children's book illustration, a craft she has been pursuing professionally for two years but has loved for a lifetime. Growing up, Sommer was drawn to the illustrations in storybooks, treasures that she cherishes to this day.

Today, Sommer creates artworks that grasp the innocence and curiosity of childhood. Her work aims to be a gentle nudge to look closer at the stories and details around them, to find values in the whimsical nature of life.

Looking ahead, Sommer wishes her illustrations to resonate with both children and adults, crafting scenes that are as enchanting to a four-year-old as they are meaningful to a forty-year-old.

Other Books in the Series

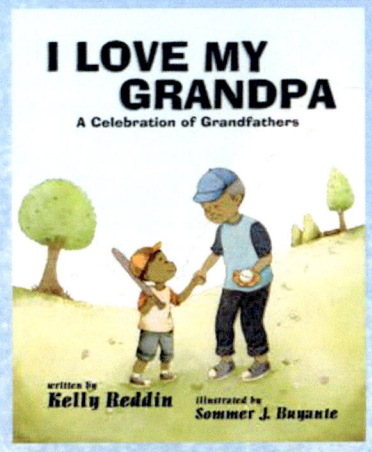
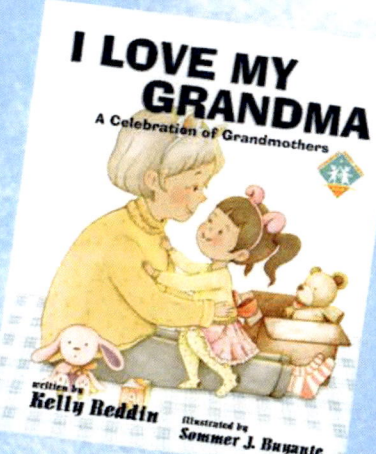
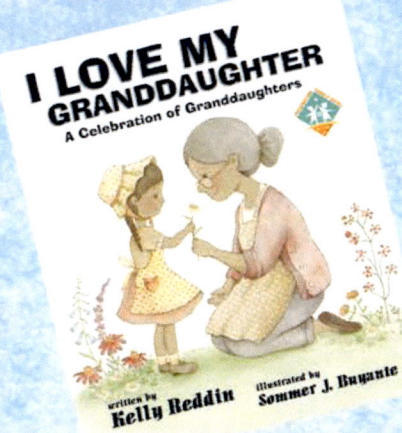

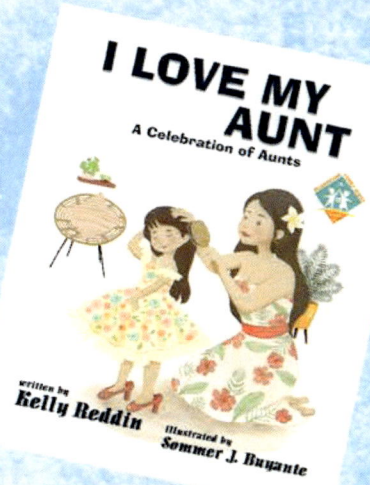

www.ingramcontent.com/pod-product-compliance
Lightning Source LLC
LaVergne TN
LVRC092314110526
838202LV00108B/2625